PRAISES FOR WALKING THROUGH GRIEF

Jesus said, "Blessed are those who mourn, for they will be comforted." Everyone will confront various experiences of grief in life. However, when we walk through our grief in the presence of our living, resurrected Lord and Savior Jesus, we will find His comfort. Brian and Leah Foutz have taken that walk through the untimely death of their daughter.

In *Walking through Grief: A Journey of Peace*, Brian provides a simple and practical explanation of how he and his wife Leah found the comfort and blessing that Jesus speaks of. He takes you through the dark shadows of mournfulness and moves you to the comfort and blessing of our Lord's light. Brian's book is redundant with reminders and filled with reflective scriptures for you to utilize in the grieving process.

Whether you are going through the process of mourning a loss or you know someone who is, this a great ministry tool for any Christian to have close by.

Dennis Keen
Pastor, West End Baptist Church
Industry, Texas

Brian and Leah have written a very personal and positive book about how they grieved after the tragic death of their daughter. They poured their hearts out on every page by sharing their own story of grief and how they came to have peace in the midst of their tragedy.

This book is something that is needed and can be used by anyone who is grieving. I would recommend their story to pastors, chaplains, or professional counsellors. Their approach to sharing their journey to peace is a powerful and honest look at the subject of grief. People need to know that they are not alone in their personal tragedy. I believe that Brian and Leah, through their writings, have paved the way for others to find peace, hope, and victory through Jesus Christ.

Linda Sensat, LPC
Burton, Texas

Only the great grace of the Lord could have accomplished what this book has defined for those who truly have and are walking through the valley of the shadow of death in losing a loved one. Brian has captured the real essence exactly as God's Word has been the meaningful solution for his and Leah's overcoming solution to life's tragedies. The most impressive is their complete dependence upon Him and the Lord doing what He does best for His children. This is a book for all mankind in their struggles with loss, not just the body of Christ.

Pastor Lynn Burling
Christian Faith Church
Bellville, Texas

WALKING THROUGH GRIEF

A Journey of Peace

Blessings,
Leah

Brian

WALKING THROUGH GRIEF

A Journey of Peace

BRIAN & LEAH FOUTZ

© 2017 by Brian Foutz. All rights reserved.

Published by Redemption Press, PO Box 427, Enumclaw, WA 98022

Toll Free (844) 2REDEEM (273-3336)

Redemption Press is honored to present this title in partnership with the author. The views expressed or implied in this work are those of the author. Redemption Press provides our imprint seal representing design excellence, creative content, and high quality production.

No part of this publication may be reproduced, stored in a retrieval system, or transmitted in any way by any means—electronic, mechanical, photocopy, recording, or otherwise—without the prior permission of the copyright holder, except as provided by USA copyright law.

Scripture quotations marked AMP are taken from the Amplified Bible, Copyright © 1954, 1958, 1962, 1964, 1965, 1987 by The Lockman Foundation. Used by permission.

Scripture quotations marked KJV are taken from the Holy Bible, King James Version, © 1979, 1980, 1982 by Thomas Nelson, Inc., Publishers. Used by permission.

Scripture quotations marked NKJV are taken from the New King James Version. Copyright © 1982 by Thomas Nelson, Inc. Used by permission. All rights reserved.

Scripture quotations marked NASB are taken from the New American Standard Bible® (NASB), Copyright © 1960, 1962, 1963, 1968, 1971, 1972, 1973, 1975, 1977, 1995 by The Lockman Foundation. Used by permission. www.Lockman.org

Scripture quotations marked NIV are taken from the Holy Bible, New International Version®, NIV® Copyright ©1973, 1978, 1984, 2011 by Biblica, Inc.® Used by permission. All rights reserved worldwide.

Scripture quotations marked NLT are taken from the Holy Bible, New Living Translation, copyright © 1996, 2004, 2015 by Tyndale House Foundation. Used by permission of Tyndale House Publishers Inc., Carol Stream, Illinois 60188. All rights reserved.

ISBN 13: 978-1-68314-502-8 (Paperback)
978-1-68314-503-5 (ePub)
978-1-68314-504-2 (Mobi)

Library of Congress Catalog Card Number: 2017957330

Contents

Foreword xi
Preface xiii
Acknowledgments xv
Introduction xix
Our Story 21
The Journey 25
What Is Grief? 31
Stages and Steps of Loss 39
Things to Ponder 49
An Interview with Leah 59
Dos and Don'ts 79

Seeking Help 85
An Interview with Brian. 89
Finding Peace in Your Life 109
A Story of Inspiration. 117
Finding Your Next Assignment. 129

FOREWORD

There have only been a handful of people in my life who truly live the life of overcomers, despite having been dealt a massive, emotional blow that no one should endure. My dear friends, Brian and Leah Foutz, fit that description and live an abundant, rewarding life that most can only aspire to achieve. Their testimony is saturated with inspiring story after inspiring story, bringing glory to the one who brought them out of darkness into His marvelous light. When one hears their story, asks the questions, and hears firsthand the inner peace and strength exemplified by Brian and Leah, despite the unfathomable loss of their only daughter, Victoria, it paints a tapestry of God's love, compassion, peace, forgiveness, and joy available to each of us, no matter the situation or circumstance.

I am proud to call Brian and Leah my friends, and I stand amazed at their resilience and positive attitudes in spite of all they have endured.

Joey Garza
www.fullmeasureproductions.com

PREFACE

If you would like to contact Brian and Leah, or would like to have them come and speak at your church or special event, you can contact them through their website at www.Hazakministries.com.

In their first book, *From Misery to Ministry: A Walk of Faith*, they began to experience unique and divine encounters that would change their lives forever, as well as the lives of those they encountered. These encounters would become the stepping stones for their own steps of faith—learning to trust Him *in* all things and *for* all things.

Their second book, *Steps of Faith*, is an exciting adventure into learning to be led by the Holy Spirit. After the loss of their only child in 2004, Brian and Leah began a journey into helping others take baby steps of faith toward healing.

Brian and Leah will bless you with their message of encouragement and help you to be open, willing, and obedient to be used by the Lord.

In *Walking through Grief: A Journey of Peace*, Brian and Leah will help you learn to find that "peace that goes beyond all understanding." It all starts by asking the Lord for help.

Acknowledgments

In all your ways know, recognize, and acknowledge
Him and He will direct and make straight and plain
your paths. (Prov. 3:6 AMP)

Leah and I have learned so much in the last eleven years since the passing of our only child, Victoria Carol Foutz. It only seems like yesterday, but it has been a season or two. Some of the material in this book has been made possible by a number of professional people who assisted us during our time of grief.

A special thanks to Rev. Mark Anderson for his counseling, love, and passion. You made it possible for us to make the transition of losing our only child easier.

To the officers and staff of Fort Bend County, the Crime Victims Fund of Fort Bend County, Texas, and for the trauma counseling it provided from Carolyn Rowe, MA, LPC of Sugarland, Texas.

Thank you to Melinda Ginter for your continued prayers and support from you and your family. And a special mention to all of you who walked with us through the death of Victoria. There have been so many of you that we just cannot mention here.

Leah and I were deeply appreciative of everyone's help, love, and comfort through Victoria's "celebration of life service." This service brought over twenty young people to the altar for prayer and eight young people gave their lives to Jesus Christ! Praise God! We also thank you for your continued love and support through our time of grief, our restoration and preparation for ministry, and through Victoria's murder trial.

We would like to give special thanks to Diane and Steve Walker, our friends in their life group, and members

Acknowledgments

of The Fellowship at Cinco Ranch, Holy Cross Church of Sugarland, Pastor Alex Kennedy of Carmel Baptist Church NC, Kingsland Baptist Church Katy, TX, Pastor Jim Leggett and Grace UMC Katy, TX, Pastors Lynn and Linda Burling and members of Christian Faith Church Bellville, TX, and my fellow Christian musicians of The Daystar Project Band and ministry, and good friends, Anthony Hall and Joey Garza.

INTRODUCTION

Since writing our first book, From Misery to Ministry: A Walk of Faith through the Loss of a Loved One, Leah and I have been asked on several occasions, "Do you and Leah have a book on helping someone go through the grief process?"

When ministering to those who have lost a loved one, we have always recommended that a person go and get professional counseling to assist them during this time of grief. We share with them that we are not licensed counselors and can only share with them on how we walked through the grief process. Since then, we have been asked several times if we had a book, based upon on our own walk, on how to walk through a time of grieving.

Over the last several years, we have been compiling our walk, thoughts, and real-life stories on how we have managed the time of learning to live with the loss of a loved one. We have written this book to share with you how we handled the grief process, and we have found peace from this journey.

May you be richly blessed and comforted from our experiences, and may this book help you to walk through grief toward a journey of peace.

Our Story

Then the Lord answered me and said, "Write the vision and engrave it plainly on [clay] tablets So that the one who reads it will run. For the vision is yet for the appointed [future] time it hurries toward the goal [of fulfillment]; it will not fail. Even though it delays, wait [patiently] for it, because it will certainly come; it will not delay.

Hab. 2:2–3 AMP

We have heard it stated over the years that when something terrible happens, out of your greatest tragedy, God will pull you up out of the ashes and renew your spirit. We have also heard that out of your greatest misery, God will birth your greatest ministry.

Leah and I have learned that out of your misery, God will bring about a time of restoration and rest. When He is ready, this can be followed by a time of preparation. Whoa! But one may ask, "Brian, what is this time of preparation? What does that look like?"

I like to share with people that when you are born, the Lord gives you certain gifts and talents. We may very well know exactly what they are and learn to use them. But as we found out later, there were some gifts that we had that we did not know we had and when ready, the Lord provided a dream and a vision to show us what He had in store for us next.

As my friend Mary Priddy once asked me, "Brian, did you ever think that you would be doing what you are doing now?" To which I replied, "This was not on my bucket list. In fact, it wasn't even anywhere near the top ten, twenty, or top fifty!"

In my thirties, I thought I would be in financial planning, helping make an impact in people's lives with their finances. In my forties that dream was still alive and thriving. In my early fifties, a change in my health began a change of direction into music and recording. At the age of fifty-four, change happened again, but this time more severely. It was not a loss of my health that changed, but the loss of our only daughter and child, Victoria, to a murder.

Devastation and not knowing what I would do next became the order of the day. But, instead of emptiness and anger and loss of willpower to work, the Lord provided another gift. From this tragedy I would be blessed with a new gift, one of encouragement. This gift would help others and give them hope and encouragement from the scriptures and our Lord.

In a dream thirty months later, the Lord would provide another new gift, the gift of writing. The thought of me writing anything was never at the forefront of my mind. In fact, I even hated to have to write letters to people. Just ask my wife, Leah. She had to write all of my letters in the early years of my insurance career.

From this came our first book, *From Misery to Ministry: A Walk of Faith*. Out of the ashes, God would birth a new ministry called Hazak Ministries. *Hazak* is a Hebrew word which means strength and encouragement. That vision He placed in our hearts was to bring a message of hope, healing, and encouragement to a lost and hurting world.

Be ready. There is a gift waiting for you!

THE JOURNEY

And my God shall supply all your need according
to His riches in glory by Christ Jesus.
(Phil. 4:19 NKJV)

After the loss of our only daughter, we began reading a number of books dealing with grief and the loss of a loved one. It has been interesting to read and see just how many different types of grief that one can go through. There are different steps and stages that one can go through as well. But what was really interesting for us is that during the entire grieving process, it was

God's answer to our prayer that really made all of the difference. That prayer was for God's peace. It is that peace that goes beyond all understanding.

> Do not be anxious about anything, but in every situation, by prayer and petition, with thanksgiving, present your requests to God. And the peace of God, which transcends all understanding, will guard your hearts and your minds in Christ Jesus.
> (Phil. 4:6–7 NIV)

After Victoria's death, we went through many emotions, pains, and struggles but His presence was always there. The Lord's presence was by us, around us, and within us. It was during this time that we realized that we would be going through a period of restoration and then later preparation.

Finding strength to persevere daily and finding that His peace will sustain you through your day is what will help you make it through the pain of loss. Learning as you go and grow through this process that the Lord has purposed for you, He will give you great comfort and joy.

The things you have learned and received and heard and seen in me, practice these things, and the God of peace will be with you.

(Phil. 4:9 NASB)

Learning to Understand the Stages of Loss

Leah and I have found that one of the most important things in understanding loss and the stages for grief can be found in scripture. Yes, there are lots of professionals and counsellors out there to help you in the process, but for us, understanding that process is found in God's Word.

You see, there is a time for everything, and there is a season for all things. Not just one thing but for all things. Here is a great reminder of God's Word in the process:

> There is a time for everything, and a season for every activity under the heavens: a time to be born and a time to die, a time to plant and a time to uproot, a time to kill and a time to heal, a time to tear down and a time to build, a time to weep and a time to laugh, a time to mourn and a time to dance, a time to scatter stones and a time to gather them, a time

to embrace and a time to refrain from embracing, a time to search and a time to give up, a time to keep and a time to throw away, a time to tear and a time to mend, a time to be silent and a time to speak, a time to love and a time to hate, a time for war and a time for peace.

(Eccles. 3:1–8 NIV)

It is interesting that God used Solomon to write this amazing chapter in the book of Ecclesiastes. We learn that God appoints the times and the seasons, He knows the date of our birth and our death, and that all things occur and happen under Him. He is all-knowing, the maker of heaven and earth, omnipotent, the beginning and the end. Basically God knows everything.

He knows when we are sleeping, when we are awake, and when have been bad or good. No, He is not Santa Claus. He is our Lord of lords and King of kings! God knows when we are hurting, when we are sad and lonely, and He gives us that answer in Matthew.

Come to Me, all who are weary and heavy-laden, and I will give you rest. Take My yoke upon you and learn from Me, for I am gentle and humble in heart, and you will find rest for your souls. For My yoke is easy and My burden is light.

(Matt. 11:28–30 NASB)

- So when we have someone close to us die, how are we supposed to feel?
- Are there stages of emotions that we go through?
- Are there any lists for these emotions?
- Do we go through them in order?
- Do we experience every one of them?
- How long do these emotions last?
- What should we do now?
- Who do we talk to?
- Where do we look for help?

Well, first things first. Before you jump into the water, you need to learn to swim. You need to take lessons and get instructions. Life is the same way. Yeah, you can jump in, but without instructions you will hit obstacles, get hurt, get into trouble, and just waste a great deal of your time. We have found that when we need help, you have to call on someone to rescue you.

No, you don't call the *Ghostbusters*!

You call on the one person who knows everything and ask Him for help. "My help comes from the Lord, Who made heaven and earth."
> (Ps. 121:2 NKJV)

In the following chapters, we will be sharing a list of things that you might experience and that you could emotionally feel. They may or may not apply to everybody, but we have tried to list the ones that we feel are most important. As my bride likes to say, "feelings are neither right nor wrong, they are just feelings."

We all have them, and we all feel different when things happen to us, both good and bad. But in the long run, it's how you handle them that counts.

When we share with you things that you might go through, remember, besides asking for help from the Lord, you also need to ask for help from professional licensed counsellors as well. We were told to get help from both the Lord and counsellors. It is one of the best things that we ever did in life!

WHAT IS GRIEF?

He heals the brokenhearted and binds up their wounds [healing their pain and comforting their sorrow].

(Ps. 147:3 AMP)

Leah and I wanted to spend time in this chapter to explain what grief is.

This is where I would like to say that we are not licensed counsellors, and we are not giving you advice or counsel—only that we are sharing with you what we have learned through our own real-life experiences. Our only daughter had been murdered, and, with the Lord's help, we began walking through grief into a journey of peace.

Here are some simple truths that we share with others about grief:

Webster's dictionary defines *grief* as a deep sadness, caused especially by someone's death, or as trouble or annoyance, or a cause for suffering or loss.

Now that word in Hebrew is *ra'ah*, and it means: bad, malignant, unpleasant, evil, displeasing, unkind, misery, distress. One thing that we wanted to share with you about grief is this, you are not the first person to feel grief nor will you be the last person. And as we have learned, with God's help, you can walk through grief and have a journey of peace.

There is this great reminder of God's promise to take care of us through our time of pain and suffering:

> And the Lord God prepared a gourd, and made it to come up over Jonah, that it might be a shadow over his head, to deliver him from his grief. So Jonah was exceeding glad of the gourd.
>
> (Jon. 4:6 KJV)

What Is Grief?

You might wonder and ask, *Okay, Brian, this sounds okay but really, why did God provide a gourd for Jonah? Isn't that something like a vegetable, you know, a squash?*

That's what I thought when I first read this. So, I decided to go and look up this word *gourd* and found something very interesting in the *Easton's Bible Dictionary*. I think you might like this:

Jonah's gourd in Jonah 4:6–10 bears the Hebrew name *kikayon* (found only here), probably the kiki of the Egyptians, the croton. This is the castor-oil plant, a species of ricinus, the palma Christi, so called from the palmate division of its leaves. Others with more probability regard it as the cucurbita, the el-keroa of the Arabs, a kind of pumpkin peculiar to the East.

"It is grown in great abundance on the alluvial banks of the Tigris and on the plain between the river and the ruins of Nineveh." At the present day it is trained to run over structures of mud and brush to form boots *to protect the gardeners from the heat of the noon-day sun.* It grows with extraordinary rapidity, and when cut or injured withers away also with great rapidity.

So, if you think about it, just as the Lord provided a gourd (a plant or vine) to protect the farmers from the heat, God can give you a covering over your head to protect you from your grief! Just as He did for Leah and me in our time of grief, God gave us a covering to protect our hearts and minds from the pain, misery, and discomfort of the loss of our only child. Now, how cool is that?!

Types of Grief

There are all types of grief that we can experience in our life due to a loss of some kind. Here is just a short list. Some of these things we have personally experienced:

- The loss of a child or another loved one (spouse, mother, father, etc.)
- The loss of health—two car accidents in two years changed both my physical and my mental health as well. Not only did I lose something, but my wife and daughter also lost the husband and dad they knew.

What Is Grief?

- Losing a home—either by default, losing a job, bankruptcy, fire, or an act of nature.
- Losing a job or business—this can be due to health, illness, downturn in the economy, no money, no business, etc.
- Having a miscarriage—or losing a baby during or after birth.
- Losing retirement or savings
- Losing a job either by downturns, business closing, or being forced into retirement early.
- Loss of friendship
- Losing self-respect and integrity

You can also feel these same things as a result of moving to another town, moving from your home or moving to another state either for business, school, or to take care of an ailing relative.

Everyone Will Grieve Differently

Here is a good thing to remember. Everyone, yes everyone, will grieve differently. Not only in the life insurance business but being a deacon at a church and in our many years in ministry, I learned that everyone has grieved differently.

There are many lists out there that will tell you what you might go through and feel. I looked at one book that listed about twenty-five things that you could go through and feel, and I have to tell you that there is no order to the number of things that you will experience. I have known people to have experienced almost all of the things on the list, and others only a handful. It all depends upon the person and how they handle the loss. And, more importantly, in whom they get help from and what they do with that help.

Ask for Help

I cannot emphasize enough that you need to get help, and especially ask for help from the Lord. This was the only way that Leah and I have made it through the storms in life.

Talk with your pastor or priest or rabbi. Talk with a close family member or friend, seek out professional help. They say that there are two things in life that bring about death and illness—these are stress and trauma.

What Is Grief?

You need to ask for help, and the number on our list was God.

> He who dwells in the shelter of the Most High will remain secure and rest in the shadow of the Almighty [whose power no enemy can withstand]. I will say of the LORD, "He is my refuge and my fortress, My God, in whom I trust [with great confidence, and on whom I rely]!" For He will save you from the trap of the fowler, and from the deadly pestilence. He will cover you and completely protect you with His pinions, and under His wings you will find refuge; His faithfulness is a shield and a wall. You will not be afraid of the terror of night, Nor of the arrow that flies by day.
>
> (Ps. 91:1–5 AMP)

Keep It Simple

Take life with one step at a time and one day at a time. These are what I like to call baby steps. When you do, you will be just fine. If possible, take as much time as you need to begin your walk through grief.

Walking Through Grief

We learned from our drives out on the roads of Texas that it is not about the distance you drive but the journey. The same thing should apply to you in your walk of grief. With God's help, this can be a journey of peace.

I love what my wife, Leah, shares with people with regard to loss and grief. She reminds them of her walk that things will get better, but they will never be okay.

STAGES AND STEPS OF LOSS

The LORD is close to the brokenhearted and saves those who are crushed in spirit.

(Ps. 34:18 NIV)

What's happening to me? I feel like everything is spinning around me, and I am tumbling down the side of a mountain! Losing a loved can be very taxing and hard, and the loss of a child seems to be the worst loss of all. For Leah and me, we found that our emotions were all over the place! Literally like a roller coaster! I don't just mean a typical roller coaster ride, but one that seemed like a Steven Spielberg and Walt Disney World movie ride.

This roller coaster is not one that you get to watch and check out before you get on, because each ride is different for every person who goes through the loss. This ride goes up and over mountains, through tunnels, jungles, desert, and in the air. There are so many twists and turns that each one seems different, and there are times that you feel like you are on a slow-moving river. And then out of nowhere, you are rushing down white-water rapids and find yourself in free fall from a waterfall and back to a slow-moving river. Suddenly you are in the ocean, rising and falling with small waves. Then you are in a huge storm almost like a tsunami, and you come crashing down on the surface and are thrown onto the beach. As you are pulled back out into the ocean, you encounter small waves, and then you are once again lifted up and onto the sand on the beach.

This is how our emotions came to us daily. There was no warning or preparation for the rush of tears that came.

At times we were very sad, other times we reflected on the joyful times of our life with our daughter. Then

STAGES AND STEPS OF LOSS

the pain would come back, sometimes just ever so lightly and others like a huge hurricane.

Our friend France Brown once shared, "Be prepared in life because you are either in a storm, just coming out of a storm, or fixin' to go into a storm!"

We want to share with you in this chapter some of the emotions and feelings that you will encounter during your time as you go through the process of grief.

Food for thought, we have tried to share a number of emotions on our list and wanted to give you something special to ponder on and remember.

There are more emotions that you could feel and go through than what we have listed here. If we missed something, it was not done on purpose.

1. There is *no order* on these feelings. These feelings will probably not happen in this order.
2. You may or may not feel all of these. You could possibly go through all of these feelings. You might experience a good number of these on the list or just a few. Again, it will really depend upon each person.

With that, here is our list of possible stages and steps of grief. *Remember, we are not licensed professional counsellors, and we are not giving any professional advice, only sharing the feelings of what we went through. Please seek professional help for counselling.*

Shock

This just can't be happening! This is our only daughter! Hint: Get help quickly.

Call your pastor or priest or rabbi. Ask for help

Call your best friend. Ask for help

Call your closest family member. Ask for help.

Denial

Denying that the loss has happened, even thinking that it was someone else. As Leah put it, "It can't be my daughter, Victoria. It had to be Brian!"

Horror

Disbelief. Why would anyone want to kill our daughter? We all have faults, but she was so loving, kind,

Stages and Steps of Loss

and compassionate, always wanting to make a friend and be *your* best friend.

Anger

You may be angry at the person who died or someone who may have been involved in the death. How could they have done this? Maybe they took their own life, crashed a vehicle or something else that resulted in their death, or another person possibly could have been at fault. We may possibly want to direct our anger at "something" or "someone."

Bargaining

You possibly may be trying to bargain with God to bring the person back. "Lord, I'll do anything if…"

Depression

This will come about from the loneliness and isolation you may be feeling, withdrawing from others. You may find yourself dwelling on the death and loss and nothing else. It is at this point that you are beyond your limit of trying to cope.

Acceptance

Learning to adapt and cope with the fact that the loss is real and facing the reality that what or who you love is no longer here.

Seek Professional Help

This is really important. You have to seek out professional help. This may include your pastor, a professional counselor, and a grief support group.

Time of Restoration

This is a time that the Lord will take you through, a time of restoring things in your life. For us, it was our marriage. For others it could be their marriage, their family, or putting your life back together.

Period of Preparation

You have lost something or someone. As you begin to heal from the loss, God will begin to prepare you for something greater than you had been doing. This is a time of great reflection and dreaming and asking Him to guide you and set you back on a path for your future.

Stages and Steps of Loss

Finding Purpose in Life

We all want to be something or be someone. We want to do something that will bring us joy and fulfillment. As a person once said, find something that you love to do, and you will never work another day in your life.

You see, we are all made in the Father's perfect image, and upon our birth He gave us gifts and talents, and He gave us a purpose in life. This is the time to seek Him out and ask Him what you were made to do. If you ask Him, He will show you what you were made to do, and you will find purpose and reason to live life to the fullest.

So what are some other things that we might be asking ourselves during this time of loss? Here are just a few things that Leah and I found ourselves talking about at Victoria's death:

What Do I Do Now?

I remembered the old line from a children's Bible program: First we pray! I asked the Lord for His help and divine intervention.

Hint: Cry out to God and ask for His help, wisdom, and His supernatural peace.

Hint: Call your home church or local funeral home.

Hint: If you have life insurance, call your agent.

What Do I Need to Do?

Since I am a type A personality and a take-charge kind of guy, I do well in chaotic situations. I bring organization out of chaos. Also, I had been in the life insurance business for over seventeen years and had handled these types of "challenges" when they came up for my policyholders and clients. Thankfully I had been well-trained and mentored in this area. In fact, there had been a number of times where I worked with my clients to call their relatives, take them to the funeral home, help them with their funeral arrangements, and yes, even fill out the paperwork for the death claim with their insurance companies. And there were times that I actually delivered the death claim check for the proceeds from the life insurance policy.

Hint: Call your church or pastor, a friend, and your life insurance agent (if you have life insurance.

Who Is Going to Help Me?

God was so good to us. He provided someone from our church to handle the meals and supplies needed for the home. Not only was there plenty of food, drinks, coffee, etc., they even brought a case of toilet paper and a case of Kleenex to our home. Now there was a gift and provision from God.

Hint: Reach out to friends and ask for help. You may be surprised and find out that there is one or more people who can help you. And remember *do not* be afraid to ask for help.

What about the Funeral Home?

This was already handled for us. Someone from our church had contacted the funeral home and arranged a quiet meeting for me to come by and plan a memorial service for us.

Where Should We Go to Have a Funeral?

Most people choose their home church or funeral home. This was easy for us because we chose the church that our daughter had grown up in for over ten years.

Hint: Call your pastor, friend, or someone that you know.

What about the Service Itself? Who Do We Call? Who Do We Use?

Hint: Call your pastor, church, friend, or professional counsel.

Again, the Lord provided for all of this. The funeral home took care of most of this. Since our daughter was cremated (a decision we had made early on), the funeral home provided the ushers, and we had friends who took care of everything else.

For us, I asked our ministry band to play for the worship service because this would be a celebration of life service, a send-off to heaven. For us, we knew that our daughter had made a profession of faith, and we knew where she was—in heaven with Jesus.

For I satisfy the weary ones and refresh everyone who languishes.

(Jer. 31:25 NASB)

Things to Ponder

> For the ways of man are before the eyes of the Lord,
> and He ponders all of his paths.
>
> (Prov. 5:21 NKJV)

Leah and I found that after the loss of our daughter, Victoria, we spent a great deal of time talking with others, just thinking about everything that was going on around us. We wanted to use this chapter to give you some ideas to think about during your time of grieving.

Walking Through Grief

First, what does the word *ponder* really mean? Well, according to Webster's dictionary, *ponder* means to think about something carefully, soberly, and deeply. Over in the King James Dictionary it means to consider carefully or meditate.

Now this word, *ponder*, in Hebrew is the word *pa-las* and it means to make level, balance, or make smooth. Here are some really great ideas to think about while you are walking through the process of grief. May your walk be a journey of peace.

So, here are seven simple things to "ponder on."

1. You need help. Realize that you need help. Ask God to help you. Pray for the peace of God, and He will give it to you.

   And the peace of God, which surpasses all understanding, will guard your hearts and minds through Christ Jesus.

   (Phil. 4:7 NKJV)

2. Why me? It is not you. And remember that you are not the first person to go through a painful

Things to Ponder

loss. Read about others who have gone through a loss and learn how they handled their grief.

Ask the Lord to bring others to you to help you walk through your own stages of grief.

No temptation has overtaken you but such as is common to man; and God is faithful, who will not allow you to be tempted beyond what you are able, but with the temptation will provide the way of escape also, so that you will be able to endure it.

(1 Cor. 10:13 NASB)

3. Do not be afraid to ask someone to pray for you and your family. When asked if it was useless to bother God with their troubles, the late evangelist D. L. Moody replied, "Some people think God does not like to be troubled with our constant coming and asking. The way to trouble God is not to come at all."

Ask for help. There are people waiting to help you through your time of need. God has already lined them up for you. Just ask.

Walking Through Grief

> Yet the LORD longs to be gracious to you; therefore he will rise up to show you compassion. For the LORD is a God of justice. Blessed are all who wait for him! People of Zion, who live in Jerusalem, you will weep no more. How gracious he will be when you cry for help! As soon as he hears, he will answer you.
>
> (Isa. 30:18–19 NIV)

Let others bless you during this time of grief. Thank the Lord for bringing them to you and ask Him to bless them and their families.

Your emotions and feelings will rise and fall like the waves of the ocean. Some waves will come like small rippling of waves rolling onto a beautiful sandy beach. Others will come crashing in like a raging storm or typhoon. Others may be somewhere in between. Realize also that there will be no warning, no flags, or sirens to tell you that the waves are approaching. They will just come and when they do, ride the wave out. Do not try to fight it or hold back

Things to Ponder

the tears. Just ride the wave. This is God's way of cleansing and healing the body.

4. Learn that there is a list of possible things you will go through and feel during your loss. It is a large list but there is no order to the list, and you may feel and go through some of them, or most of them, possibly even all of them, but there is no order in which this will happen.

   Consider it all joy, my brethren, when you encounter various trials, knowing that the testing of your faith produces endurance. And let endurance have its perfect result, so that you may be perfect and complete, lacking in nothing.
   (James 1:2–4 NASB)

5. Realize that there is a process of walking through grief. If you are like me, I hate the process. It sucks but there is a process, and you have to learn to embrace this so that you can heal.

> For everything that was written in the past was written to teach us, so that through the endurance taught in the Scriptures and the encouragement they provide we might have hope.
>
> (Rom. 15:4 NIV)

6. This time is a period of restoration and preparation for you.

> And the God of all grace, who called you to his eternal glory in Christ, after you have suffered a little while, will himself restore you and make you strong, firm and steadfast.
>
> (1 Pet. 5:10 NIV)

Know that through this process, God is taking you through a period of restoration and preparation. The restoration period is repairing the brokenness in your life—the loss of a loved one, repairing your heart, repairing your family, the brokenness that you and your spouse or children may have, and restoring other things

Things to Ponder

that you love in life. As you are being restored, God will begin to give you a vision for your future and show you ideas that will help you find a new purpose in life. This may very well be something that you never thought you would do and something (at that moment) that you think you are not capable of doing. His vision is greater than anything you could think of, and He will provide everything that you will need to accomplish His vision for your life.

7. Learn to take baby steps. Just like a small baby, you will learn to crawl and then walk. During this time, you may feel like giving in and giving up but don't! Don't quit. There is hope. God will fill that emptiness, and He will give you a reason to live. Choose life!

Take small steps each day to get better. You may not be able to do *all* that you are used to doing, and that is okay. Take baby steps to begin your walk through grief.

Find something that you like to do and do that. This will help you and encourage you to take the next baby step.

Here is something very important to remember. We have to walk by faith.

> Now faith is the substance of things hoped for, the evidence of things not seen.
>
> (Heb.11:1 NKJV)

We have to learn that the Lord can restore all things.

> And without faith it is impossible to please God, because anyone who comes to him must believe that he exists and that he rewards those who earnestly seek him.
>
> (Heb. 11:6 NIV)

Learn to do new things, fun things, things that will let you be creative. These will give you reasons for living, for becoming productive, and for finding purpose again in life. Some examples may be: drawing, painting, playing, writing music, gardening, canning fruits and vegetables, writing poems, fishing, hiking, playing golf

Things to Ponder

or another sport, serving and helping others, taking groceries to someone, and helping at your church or a local organization where you live.

God has great things in store for you my friend. Bill Adams, a friend of mine, once told me that pain is temporary, but quitting is forever.

I want to leave you this one verse, to encourage you to be strong. In Hebrew, that word strong is *Hazak*. Take strength in the Lord, seek Him out, and He will provide all things!

> And the God of all grace, who called you to his eternal glory in Christ, after you have suffered a little while, will himself restore you and make you strong, firm and steadfast.
>
> (1 Pet. 5:10 NIV)

An Interview with Leah

Praise be to the God and Father of our Lord Jesus Christ, the Father of compassion and the God of all comfort, who comforts us in all our troubles, so that we can comfort those in any trouble with the comfort we ourselves receive from God.

(2 Cor. 1:3–4 NIV)

Leah and I had been praying on how we might share with you some of the things that one might go through during the grief process. After much prayer, we felt a prompting in our spirit to do something a little different. Instead of just writing our thoughts out and putting them in a story line, we felt that it would be neat to share these thoughts in an interview format.

You know, just like when you read an interview in a magazine or newspaper article. So most of the time, we can share about our story and think we know what the other person is going through, even when you are walking right beside them.

After much prayer, Leah decided that she would like for me to be the one to do the interview with her. After some more time in prayer, the Lord gave me the questions to ask her. I was honored to do this, and I was surprised to learn things that I had not realized or ever asked of my bride.

Upon finishing my interview with her, we knew this was how the Lord wanted us to write this chapter. So, here is my interview with Leah.

Brian: Leah, thank you for being available to take this time to share with others what was in your heart during the time when you lost Victoria.

An Interview with Leah

Leah: Thank you, my prayer is that this interview will be helpful to our readers. That this will bring hope, healing, and encouragement to them; and that they will receive a blessing!

Brian: While I was preparing for this interview, one question that I had was, "How did you feel when you first heard about the news of Victoria's death?"

Leah: I was working at a temporary job assignment in west Houston when two ladies and our pastor from our church came to my office. They asked if they could talk to me, and we moved down the hall to the president's office. He was not in that day, and this would be a quiet area for them to talk to me. It was at that point that they told me that Victoria had died.

Brian: Wow! That must have been horrible! How did you feel?

Leah: Devastated! I felt like my whole world crashed around me. I was caught in a giant whirlpool, spinning out of control, and getting further and further under a giant wave, crashing over and around me!

Brian: Devastated. Now there is a word that I had not thought of!

Leah: I felt so numb . . . so much pain . . . so lost. I could not believe that Victoria was dead. My very first thoughts were that the friends who came to tell me were mistaken. *It MUST have been BRIAN that they meant. Children should NEVER die before their parents. It's not the "correct" order of things!*

It was so frightening. As if someone or something had reached down, plucked me up, and viciously threw me into the ocean! I had trouble breathing, my heart was racing, and I felt as if I was going to faint.

An Interview with Leah

Brian: You said that you thought it was your husband, Brian?

Leah: YES! It had to be Brian. God had promised me that Victoria would come home, and that she would be the young woman that God meant for her to be. It wasn't time!

Brian: Were there any other feelings that you had at this time?

Leah: Yes. There was shock! I was stunned!

Brian: How did you feel after the first shock wave?

Leah: The first thing I did was pray. I prayed to God that this was NOT TRUE; although I suspected that it WAS true. My mind tried to get around the shock, but it wasn't working! I felt sick and faint all at the same time but could not grasp the situation either. All I could think was,

Walking Through Grief

"WHAT?!?" And then my first question was, "How is Brian? Does he know?"

Brian: From your first book, we read that Brian already knew, and that he had sent someone to help you.

Leah: Yes, that's true but at the time I did not know this. After assurances from my friends that, yes, Brian knew, I felt numbness. My mind just went blank for a moment. Tears of pain were pouring from my eyes, and my mind seemed to be frozen. I could not think!

Brian: While all of this was going on, how did you feel about Brian at this moment?

Leah: I really NEEDED to get to BRIAN as soon as possible! Somehow, I knew this was true, and all I could think was that I needed to get home to Brian as quickly as I could! I knew he would be devastated as well, and that we needed to help each other.

An Interview with Leah

Brian: So, what else were you doing, and how did you feel about the current situation and challenge that was swirling around you?

Leah: I like the way you put that—the challenge. I hear people talk about their PROBLEM or PROBLEMS all of the time, and my Brian reminds me that "there are no problems in life, only challenges!"

Brian: What a positive way to look at problems in life, to see the problems as a challenge! So what was happening with you at this time?

Leah: There were many questions swirling around in my head, and I could not think at all. I don't recall anything on the way to the house, only that it seemed to take forever to get there. When we drove into the driveway and Brian held me, my first words to him were, "Is it true? Is she really gone?" Brian said, "Yes, it is true." His answer confirmed it, and we just held each other for a while.

Brian: Did you have any other feelings at this time?

Leah: I was numb but so distraught. Victoria was my joy, my girl! She just wasn't SUPPOSED to die before Brian and me! This was not the NORMAL way that things worked!

Brian: While all of this was going on, did you have any thoughts about Brian, possibly of what he might be thinking?

Leah: My heart ached so much for Brian! Victoria was "his" girl! I knew that he was CRUSHED beyond measure!

As I shared earlier, I really NEEDED to get to BRIAN as soon as possible! Somehow, I knew this was true, and all I could think was that I needed to get home to Brian as quickly as I could!

An Interview with Leah

Brian: So, once you left the office, and you saw Brian, what did it feel like once you were home?

Leah: Boy, it was weird. That day and moving forward, it seemed like the house was shrinking as more and more friends entered our home. All of the telephones in the house were constantly ringing, and someone was answering the calls.

I later found out that it was Brian answering the house phone, office phone, and mobile phone.

Brian: Wow. He must have been busy!

Leah: Yes, he was. But he is amazing. Well-organized and calm in chaotic situations! He "held down the fort" as they say!

Brian: So what else was happening to you at home? What did you do?

Leah: I could only sit in the living room and weep, barely noticing the people who were there with me. Their condolences fell on my deaf ears. I could not think nor hear nor do anything but pray to myself.

Brian: Was there anyone there helping you at this time?

Leah: My good friend Holly Dalrymple sat next to me, quietly holding my hand most of the time while she was there. She was an amazing friend who just loved me and assisted me if I needed anything.

Brian: What else can you remember that was going on at this time?

Leah: I remember someone pushing a sandwich at me to eat and bringing me something to drink at some point. Brian was out of the living room most of the time, and I was being helped by several friends constantly. I think Brian or someone else called my temporary agency and told them what was going on. My temporary

An Interview with Leah

agency staff sent a card in a few days and told me not to worry about anything, to take care of what needed to be done.

Brian: At any point in time, were you angry at the young men who took your daughter's life?

Leah: No, I never was. The reason is that I know who roams this earth to hurt, steal, lie, cheat, deceive, and even kill people in this world. He has a name, and his name is Satan, the father of all lies! I am reminded of this in scripture,

> Be sober, be vigilant; because your adversary the devil walks about like a roaring lion, seeking whom he may devour.
> (1 Pet. 5:8 NKJV)

Brian: At any time, were you ever mad at God?

Leah: I was never mad at God.

Brian: Why is that?

Leah: Because I trust in Him. When I need Him, He tells me to call on Him. I like what it says in Psalm 18:2:

> The Lord is my rock and my fortress and my deliverer, My God, my rock, in whom I take refuge; My shield and the horn of my salvation, my stronghold.
>
> (Ps. 18:2 NASB)

Brian: Leah, you have answered some really tough questions, are you up to some more questions?

Leah: Sure, I would love to share anything that I can!

Brian: Okay. You shared with us about what was happening with you and Brian, but what about the other family members, how were they reacting or responding?

Leah: Well, Brian's family did not live in Texas, and they lived on both sides of the country. They were sorry about the loss of Victoria, but they

An Interview with Leah

were not around the corner as they say. His brother and wife sent their condolences, his oldest sister, Claudia, wanted to help out with a love offering and blessing, and his other sister, Marta, came out for a week. She helped keep the house clean with all of the visitors and took great care of Trooper, our golden retriever!

Brian: Wow! So how did your fellow workers feel at this time?

Leah: They were very sympathetic, but not close to me. One former supervisor came to the funeral. We were good friends, and he felt he needed to be there for us.

Brian: Thank you for sharing, Leah. So, how did your friends react or respond to you after Victoria passed away?

Leah: We loved so many who had been close to us over the years. With most of our family scattered across the country, our church friends had become "our family." Mostly because they were right there where we lived and worked. I had no doubts about our friends being there for us during this awful time!

Brian: Here are some questions that people have asked. What did your typical day feel like right after Victoria's death? Was there something that you did?

Leah: I think that I was mostly on "auto drive"—talking with family members, teenagers who stopped by, and the large number of friends who came by to show love and to minister to us.

Brian: Was there something that you looked forward to?

Leah: At first, I looked forward to getting past the funeral, mostly. I just wanted LIFE to get back to "normal"—at least as normal as possible.

An Interview with Leah

Brian: Was there anything else that you looked forward to?

Leah: Yes, in time, Brian and I would eat breakfast and then go for a drive. At first, they were just short drives to a small town west of Katy and back. Then later, the drives became a time that it was just Brian, me, and the Lord. These became part of our journey through the process of grief. As Briny, my name for him, would later share when driving, "It is not about the distance but the journey!"

Brian: Wow! That is really sweet.

Leah: Yes, it was, and it was something that I continue to look forward to every week. Brian will look over at me when we are out shopping or eating and then say, "Do you want to go home or go for a drive?" Sometimes I say a long drive, and then sometimes I just say a short drive. If I am not sure about which drive, I just tell him, "You choose."

Brian: When people would ask you, "How are you feeling?" what did you say to them?

Leah: I mostly told them I was "fine." I did not feel like talking much, but with so many people there caring for us, I knew I needed to be "available" for them and let them see that I was coping as well as I could.

Brian: How did you really feel when you heard this?

Leah: In the beginning, my first reaction was, "*Well, how do you THINK I'm feeling?*" But I never said that. NEVER! I knew that everyone was only trying to help and to express love for us. Inside my head I was thinking, "*What do they THINK I'm thinking?*"

Brian: So, what did you say?

An Interview with Leah

Leah: Usually I simply said I was okay and thanked them for checking on me.

Brian: What did YOU REALLY feel like saying?

Leah: At times, when I was really tired, I wanted to tell them to just shut up and leave me alone. But I never did, because they were here for me, though not really knowing what to do but show love and to be there for me. That was a nice feeling to know that God was there and that He sent these people to love me and be available if I needed them.

Brian: Okay, I have just a couple more questions for you. "How did you feel about the future at this time?"

Leah: That first day, I didn't have a single thought about the future. I don't know when Brian and I really talked about it, or if we even did.

Brian: How did this affect your time with your husband?

Leah: Brian and I had to take a good hard look at our marriage, and we both had to decide whether we even WANTED to stay together. We knew of one or two other couples who had lost a child, and they had really gone through a "rough patch." One of them got divorced shortly after losing their son. I was NOT going to let us be one of those couples who have such TINY FAITH in God that they simply give up and take the easy way out.

Brian: As time went on, were there any other thoughts about the future later?

Leah: At that time, all I could think of was getting to Brian so that we could be together through this—that we would be able to stand strong in the face of such unbelievable pain and grief. I felt, even at that time, that Brian and I

An Interview with Leah

could withstand ANYTHING with God, and that together the THREE of us would come through this trial. Wounded, yes, but ultimately triumphant!

Brian: Thank you so much for taking time out in sharing part of your life with me and our readers. I know that this will bring hope, healing, and encouragement to many people who have suffered the loss of a loved one.

Leah: You are most welcome.

Dos and Don'ts

For I have given rest to the weary and joy to the sorrowing.

(Jer. 31:25 NLT)

There are a lot of books out there with facts and fiction and what to do or not to do. As my bride, Leah, likes to say, "Feelings are just that, feelings. There is no right or wrong when you feel, because they are just feelings." A number of people have asked us over the years, "Is there a right way to feel? Is there something that I should be doing? And is there something that I shouldn't do?"

These questions are from those who have lost someone or something, and those who want to help someone who is grieving over a loss. Leah and I prayed about it while writing this book and thought we would share with you some of our thoughts. Remember, these are not right or wrong answers, only some helpful ways to assist you as you walk through grief and help others through the process.

Go with the flow. Your body will go through a number of emotions especially pain for the loss. And yes this will include crying, weeping, and mourning. These are natural responses that the body is going through. It is just one of the divine functions that the Lord uses to cleanse the body and help it to heal.

Do not try to suppress these emotions (pain and grief). If you do, it will take longer to heal and cause challenges later down the road, both mentally and physically. To heal properly over time, you will need to go through these emotions. As a man, I found that this was painful at

Dos and Don'ts

first, but over time, the Lord brought about an amazing healing for me, both mentally and physically.

Think of these emotions like waves. Yes, like waves. In the ocean, you can have small waves, ripples, or even huge storms or tsunamis that will rush onto the shoreline. Your body will experience these same types of waves.

Grief has no timetable. Yes, you read it correctly. There is no time clock for grief. There is no gauge, meter, or flowchart out there that will tell you how long you are supposed to grieve for the loss in your life. I mean, that would be great if there was, and then you be looking at this like running toward a finish line or end of a project. But there just is *no* chart for you to use. Sorry. The time to grieve will be different for each person.

Expect surprises in your emotions. Boy this was a tough one for me, but something amazing has come out of this. You may find yourself looking at something, and suddenly you have this rush of emotions about your loss. You either get angry or frustrated, or you begin to weep uncontrollably. This is part of life, and "it happens." Or as some people like to say today, "It is what it is."

> To every thing there is a season, and a time to every purpose under the heaven: a time to weep, and a time to laugh; a time to mourn, and a time to dance
> (Eccles. 3:1, 4 KJV)

There have been times that I have broken down inside of a store or office, and I have shared the story of our loss of our daughter being murdered and told of His amazing answer to prayer. I can share that peace that goes beyond all understanding and share that peace with joy! God will give you what you need when you need it.

Remember the good times and share those fond memories with others. Do not dwell on the negative or terrible things from the loss, these will only reinforce the pain, and you will never heal properly.

Learn to listen more and encourage others more. This is extremely important. If you listen long enough, people will tell you what they need, and you can help them by just listening. Sometimes, we may be around someone to help them, to minister to them, and to bless them. Do not be surprised if *you* are the one who gets the blessing!

Ask for help. This can be a very big challenge for people. Why? Because we think that we are to be strong,

Dos and Don'ts

mighty, and we do not need help. We can do it ourselves. I have news for you. You can only be strong when you ask for help.

> I will call upon the LORD, who is worthy to be praised: so shall I be saved from mine enemies.
> (Ps. 18:3 KJV)

I learned this lesson very well while going through the grief process. The more that I turned to God and leaned upon Him, the stronger that I became in overcoming this terrible loss. Yes, my help comes from the Lord!

Seeking Help

Ask, and it will be given to you; seek, and you will find; knock, and it will be opened to you
(Matt. 7:7 NKJV)

During your journey of going through the grief process, it will be important for you to ask for help. We all need help in one area or another to assist us in our grief and to help us to get back on track in life.

Should you or one of your friends or relatives find yourself needing help in coping with the loss of a loved one or another loss of some kind, ask for help. Here is a list of some of the people that you might try to contact.

Your Pastor, Priest, or Rabbi

They deal with people who have had losses, both loved ones and things. And they can pray with you and give you some guidance in dealing with your grief.

A Friend or Relative Who Has Suffered a Loss

There may be some in this category who have lost someone or something and have had some experience on what to do next.

Your Insurance Agent, Accountant, or an Attorney

Yes, this group of people will be able to help you, not only in the loss of those "material things" that you own, but especially with the loss of a loved one. In the event of death, they may be able to help you with filing death claims, taxes, and family legal planning. There may be some changes that need to be addressed, and they would be able to help you with that now.

Professional Counsellors and Doctors

This group would be able to give you professional counselling for your loss and help to establish a plan to get you back on track in life.

Seeking Help

Care Groups

This could include grief support groups, bereavement groups, Compassionate Friends*, and other groups to help assist you during the grieving process and even after. Remember, everyone grieves differently and for a different period of time.

* Note: Compassionate Friends is an organization located in Katy, Texas.*

Internet Resources

Be sure to check out any resources on the Internet to assist you with your time of grief. There are many sites to choose from and too many to share within this book. Here is our special list of those who helped us in our walk and journey.

- Linda Sensat, MS, LPC
  Christian Counsellor
  http://www.lindasensat.com

- Carolyn Rowe, LPC
  http://www.christiancounselinghouston.com/carolyn-rowe.html

An Interview with Brian

You did not choose me, but I chose you and appointed you so that you might go and bear fruit—fruit that will last and so that whatever you ask in my name the Father will give you.

(John 15:16 NIV)

Joey Garza is the owner of Full Measure Productions in Houston, Texas. He is not only a close personal friend but also a vocalist, musician, and composer. He is also an amazing sound engineer and producer. Leah and I asked Joey if he would do a live interview with me, Brian, and he accepted.

"I had the honor to sit down and interview Brian Foutz about the loss of their only daughter, Victoria. I was stunned and in awe by his responses and amazed at his peace and strength through this terrible loss. You will be blessed."

—Joey Garza

Joey: Thank you for meeting with me. I wanted to ask you some questions about your daughter, Victoria. Could you tell me what your morning was like, prior to learning about Victoria's untimely death? Can I assume that your morning was a typical one?

Brian: It was a Thursday morning, March 18th. I was having my usual breakfast meeting with my friend "Ed the Fed." Ed was a federal bank examiner but had always wanted to be an FBI agent. However, he wore glasses which kept him out of the FBI. Anyway, we were having breakfast at Chick-fil-A on Mason Road in Katy, Texas. It was our usual breakfast and time to talk and just laugh about life. Later I returned home

An Interview with Brian

and headed off to church for a music meeting with Gail, one of the singers from the praise team at church. I had a new song that I wanted to try out and wanted to have her sing this song. As it turned out, the song was beautiful. I felt like I had one of the highest highs of my life and was just floating through space.

When I returned home, I sat down at my computer to work. But there was something wrong. I had the huge feeling of oppression about me, like there was an elephant sitting on my chest. I wasn't having a heart attack or anything. It felt like I could not breathe, and it felt like a big, black cloud was covering me—a feeling of something evil in the air.

Joey: Wow! It seems as though you were sensing the situation in the spiritual realm.

Brian: Yes, it did. It was really strange. And I just couldn't put my finger on why I was feeling that way. I just couldn't shake it off. It was strange.

Walking Through Grief

Joey: How did you learn what had happened to Victoria?

Brian: Not sure of the exact time, but somewhere around 10:00 a.m. or so, I was sitting at my desk trying to work when I heard some car doors close in the driveway. I didn't even hear a car drive up. I went to the door, and two men came walking up the driveway. They had orange vests on that said "Sheriff."

Joey: So what was going through your mind as the police officers approached to tell you the grim news?

Brian: Once the sheriffs came to the door, they asked if there were any parents of Victoria Foutz at home. My first thought was, *Great Vic! What have you done now?* I invited them inside. And as it turned out, they were looking around, asking when I last saw Victoria. The questions seemed odd, and I thought they were "looking" for Victoria. Then they asked if they could sit down, and then one

An Interview with Brian

officer said, "I don't know how to tell you this, but around 6:30 a.m., Victoria's body was found on the side of the road with a gunshot wound to the head."

Joey: Is it even possible to describe the degree of mental trauma you felt at that moment?

Brian: I was in shock. The first words out of my mouth were, "Excuse me?" They repeated the news and then I said, "How do you know that it was Victoria?" One of the sheriffs replied, "We found her purse next to her body with her picture ID." I just sat there in horror. My worst fears for Victoria had come true.

Joey: Whoa! That's too much to handle. As a parent, had you previously expressed your concerns for her safety?

Brian: I used to tell her that I was worried about her and that I was afraid that, whether her fault or someone else's fault, she might be somewhere

where I would not be able to help and protect her. I think this is the "King Richard" or knight-in-shining-armor role that fathers have about their daughters. We want to be there to guide them, love them, and protect them.

Joey: What was the first thing you did? Pray? Did you call Leah? Did you call a friend?

Brian: One of my first thoughts was, *God, I don't know what to do here. I really need your help. I am praying for your wisdom and strength. Help me, God.* I also knew that I would need His help, and that I would need the help and support of friends. I first called my friend Bruce across the street, but all I got was a voice mail. Then I called Ed-the-Fed. After telling him what was going on, he said, "I'm on the way!" He hung up the phone and was there in what seemed like five minutes, but I am sure it was a little longer. But, boy! Was it quick!

Later, I had four detectives in the house, and a friend came by and said he heard the news.

An Interview with Brian

"How?" I asked. "They have been announcing it on the radio!" Then horror came over me. *My God! Leah does not know yet! She listens to the radio by her desk at work. I have to get to her and let her know but I can't leave!* I turned to Ed and said, "You have got to call the pastor to get to her work and tell her. I can't leave. I am stuck here with the detectives." Ed replied, "I'm on it!"

There was pain, shock, horror, grief, and relief—all within sixty minutes. They say that there are sixty golden seconds and sixty golden minutes. But in life, so much *can* happen in only sixty minutes! And these can be life-changing.

Joey: Can you describe your thoughts when you first saw Leah afterward?

Brian: Since I was not able to leave the house and had four detectives questioning me, I managed to get Ed-the-Fed to call our pastor and, with Ed's wife and another lady from the church, they were able to go and let Leah know what was happening. I heard weeping from outside. I got up and looked out and saw Leah walking up the drive with Mary and Diane on each side of her, holding her up as they came toward the house. I thought, *I just don't know what I can say to her, but Lord, give me the words to comfort her.*

When she came up the driveway to the house, she grabbed me, looked me in the eye and said, "Is it true?"

"Yes," I said, "it's true." We both knew at that very moment that God would have to hold everything together for us. "With man, things are impossible, but with God, ALL things are possible!"

Joey: Did anyone come to your side immediately after hearing the terrible news? You must have had friends and church members make their way to you, right?

Brian: I managed to get hold of Ed-the-Fed. He was there by my side in a flash. Shortly after that, Alan Litvak came by the house, then Barry (our worship leader from church), then Larry, one of

An Interview with Brian

Victoria's friends, came by. Then soon the house started filling up with people.

Joey: Did you ever have concerns that Victoria may be exposed to or associated with bad people?

Brian: That it would happen to me, no. But that it could happen to Victoria, yes. One of my greatest fears during her time when she was being consumed by the "dark side" was that she would get somewhere. Either by her fault or someone else's, she would find herself in a place where I could not help her. Because of some of the people that she was hanging around with, I was very concerned for her health and safety. It's a "dad thing." Sadly, that fear became a reality. We need to pray for our children daily and ask the Lord to guide them and protect them. Never stop doing this.

Joey: As a believer, how does one appropriate godly guidance for the emotional trauma you and Leah experienced?

Brian: It has been an amazing journey. On the day that Victoria was murdered, we asked the Lord to give us His grace and peace. We needed all of His help. Within forty-eight hours the Lord gave us a supernatural peace about her passing. That was the peace that goes beyond all understanding.

And the peace of God, which surpasses all comprehension, will guard your hearts and your minds in Christ Jesus.

(Phil. 4:7 NASB)

The Lord then took us through the grief process, a period of restoration of our marriage, and then preparation for ministry. During this process, the Lord began to refine me like precious silver, and reshape my character into one that would become an encourager.

During this process, Rev. France Brown of Houston brought a powerful message to our church, Grace Fellowship UMC in Katy, TX. France gave a message of hope from David and how his heart ached when he learned of

An Interview with Brian

the destruction of the town of Ziklag. It was a terrible storm for David. The message—a simple one—was that we will all face storms in our life. He said, "In life, you are either in a storm, coming out of a storm, or fixin' to head into a storm."

The Lord spoke to us and gave us a vision for our calling—to bring a message of hope, healing, and encouragement to those who are lost, hurting, or hopeless. The apostle James wrote about how to handle these storms and trials in our life:

Consider it pure joy, my brothers and sisters, whenever you face trials of many kinds, because you know that the testing of your faith produces perseverance.

(James 2:3 NIV)

We have been blessed so that we can bless others.

Joey: Did that event affect your marriage relationship?

Brian: The murder of our only child could have been the deal breaker for us and our marriage. This type of death has destroyed many marriages of those who have lost a child to a murder.

With His answered prayer of peace, and with His help, the Lord brought us closer together. We learned to depend upon each other, to talk to one another, to walk through the valley of death together—to be open, willing, and obedient to being used by Him for His glory.

Our friends began seeing a change in us, always wondering how we could have such joy and peace. And when they asked how we were doing, our reply became one of hope for others. Our answer was simple, "We are blessed!"

Joey: How did that experience help you to help others?

Brian: This experience was life-changing, and one that would start us on a new path to help others. As someone once said, "Out of the ashes God can

An Interview with Brian

restore you, and from your greatest misery, God will birth your greatest ministry."

The Lord has opened many doors for us to minister to others who have lost a loved one and to be able to share His love and message of the way.

We have been told that as Christians we should always have a testimony ready when someone asks about the Lord. Besides our testimonies of getting saved, the testimony of what God did for us during this terrible tragedy has been one that brings hope, healing, and encouragement to others.

Joey: Did that experience affect your "gift" of music in any way?

Brian: Before Victoria died, I had been playing with an awesome and talented group of musicians called The Daystar Project band. I played keyboards and arranged some songs for the group. I felt like I was really developing the talents I had been given since birth. I am an "okay" keyboardist, and I like the creative process of working on songs.

I asked the band to play for Victoria's celebration of life service. It was an amazing service. After her celebration of life service, several people were in awe of us and of me playing for the service. They just could not believe that I was able to do this. Yes, it was a God thing.

With regard to the experience of the service, I think my sister Marta said it best. She said, "Brian, I have always liked your music, but there was always something missing. I did not know what it was until the service. Today, I heard something new and different. I heard passion in your playing."

So this "passion" was the missing link in my music. This new passion began changing the way I played and felt, both in my practice time and in my writing time, and in worship. And, in the years to come, this passion could be heard in my

An Interview with Brian

playing, in the writing, and arranging, and a new heart of passion for worship took over. No longer was I playing for performance, but I was now playing for an audience of one. It is all for Him!

Joey: What advice would you give to others who have had similar traumatic experiences?

Brian: First, you pray! Ask the Lord to help you go through this storm. Ask for His grace, His love, and for His supernatural peace. Yes, that peace that goes beyond all understanding. Seek His guidance and His wisdom. Ask for help from your pastor, from your family and friends, and others. And most importantly, you have to go and get some counselling.

Read some books on grief. It will be painful, but you will learn how to cope. Also, if possible, read a book from someone who has gone through what you have gone through, and has learned to find joy in life. Find someone that you can call on who has been through your type of grief who can give you hope and encouragement.

Be prepared to ask the Lord how He can use you after this terrible ordeal. His word gives us that hope.

For whatever was written in earlier times was written for our instruction, so that through perseverance and the encouragement of the Scriptures we might have hope.
(Rom.15:4 NASB)

Joey: Did this event change your prayer life or your outlook on life itself? What about your walk with God, and your relationships with others?

Brian: Wow! That's a bunch to think about.

Joey: Yes it is, but I think people would like to know your innermost thoughts.

Brian: We learned that the death of a child is the worst thing that you will ever experience in life. You

An Interview with Brian

find that you can face anything after this, and that you seek God for His help in all things. My prayer life exploded. We began to learn that what you pray for is not about you, but about what the Lord wants you to do and what His will for your life is.

You may find yourself asking Him in prayer, "What is my purpose in life and what was I made to do?" And guess what, He will reveal that mystery to you. As my friend Joey likes to say, "It is amazing!"

My outlook on life changed totally. As I like to share with people today, I give Him praise every morning. I am thankful for another day that I am on the topside of the grass, and that I am eager to be open, willing, and obedient to be used by Him. Without Jesus Christ, I am nothing but dust, and everything else is just "stuff."

My walk with God has been learning to trust Him, to be led by the Holy Spirit and to let Him have control in my life. As I like to say now, my hands are not on the helm of the ship. His hands are on the wheel, and He navigates my path through life.

My relationship with others has greatly changed as well. I have been learning to be open to share God's word, His grace, and His love. It's not a debate about who is right or wrong. It is all about abiding in Him and being used by Him to bring Him glory.

The race in life is not about the pursuit of happiness, money, and fame, and to win the game. It is about serving Him and doing the will of Him who sent us. I love being in ministry and encouraging others.

Joey: If there was one life lesson that you learned through this experience, what would it be?

Brian: Trust in God. He will guide you and provide for you. He will never leave you nor forsake you. As the old song goes: "Trust and obey for there is no other way." With God, ALL things are possible!

An Interview with Brian

Joey: Before we wrap up, do you have any final thoughts or comments?

Brian: You know, "scholars" say that you need a positive attitude, and you can do anything that you want in life. But if you really want to live a joyful life and make an impact in this world, ask the Lord to give you a vision and a purpose. The prophet Jeremiah said it best,

> Call to Me and I will answer you, and I will tell you great and mighty things, which you do not know.
> (Jer. 33:3 NASB)

The Lord saved my wife and me from destruction and changed our life. And, out of the ashes and the misery, He birthed our greatest ministry—a ministry to bring hope, to bring healing, and to bring encouragement.

Joey: Brian, I just wanted to thank you for taking time out to share your life event with us. I know that others who will read this will be blessed and encouraged. I know that I was. Thank you again.

Brian: You are most welcome.

Finding Peace in Your Life

I have told you these things, so that in Me you may have [perfect] peace. In the world you have tribulation and distress and suffering, but be courageous [be confident, be undaunted, be filled with joy]; I have overcome the world. My conquest is accomplished, My victory abiding.

(John 16:33 AMP)

When a man's ways are pleasing to the Lord, He makes even his enemies to be at peace with him.

(Prov. 16:7 NASB)

Walking Through Grief

Over the years, we have had many people ask us these questions when learning about losing our only daughter:

"How did you find any peace?"

"How do you feel about the young men who killed your daughter?"

"Were you mad at God?"

All good questions, our friend Stephen Coffee would say. When these questions come up, here is what we share with others:

After hearing the news of Victoria, that evening we prayed to our Lord and asked Him for His help, to protect us, to feel His love, and to give us His peace. Our prayers were answered within forty-eight hours. He showed us His love by sending fellow believers in Christ to love and minister to us. Some strong men from the church came to watch over our home, and police officers sought out and found those responsible for taking our daughter's life. But the most amazing thing of all was the peace that He gave to Leah and me. It is that supernatural peace that goes beyond all understanding.

> Be anxious for nothing, but in everything by prayer and supplication, with thanksgiving, let your requests be made known to God; and the peace of God, which surpasses all understanding, will guard your hearts and minds through Christ Jesus.
>
> (Phil. 4:6–7 NKJV)

We felt sad for those men who took our daughter's life, because they, too, had lost their lives as well. But our attention was not on them, but on the one who had sent them. They were not the enemy, the enemy is Satan. He is the one who lies, cheats, deceives, and kills.

> Be of sober spirit, be on the alert. Your adversary, the devil, prowls around like a roaring lion, seeking someone to devour.
>
> (1 Pet. 5:8 NASB)

And lastly, no, we were not mad at God. We questioned God. *Why? Why her? Why now? What did we do to deserve this?* But all through the process, we knew that God was not to blame. He is a God of love. He is omnipotent and all-knowing.

> There is an appointed time for everything. And there is a time for every event under heaven.
>
> (Eccles. 3:1 NASB)

And here is something really special to remember—when you are seeking God's help, for Him to guide your thoughts and your steps, everything becomes a little easier to handle. The storm is not so bad when Jesus is in the boat!

> Then he said, I tell you the truth, unless you turn from your sins and become like little children, you will never get into the Kingdom of Heaven.
>
> (Matt. 18:3 NLT)

And speaking of heaven, I wanted to add something very special to this chapter.

People have asked us if we know where Victoria is. You know the line, "What are you going to do now, knowing that Victoria is in your past?" I am reminded of the line that Jesse Duplantis shared in one of his sermons about losing his mother, and Leah and I have used this same line to respond to others.

Finding Peace in Your Life

We know our daughter gave her life to Jesus. She lived for Him, then, she like many others fell away from Him for awhile, but she cried out to Him. He forgave her of her sins and she returned to His loving arms.

So, when we are asked this question, we love to respond and say, "Victoria is not in our past, she is in our future!"

This is the hope for all of us—to die and meet Jesus, and to be reunited with our loved ones. And here is something else really neat. We will get to meet all of those "cool guys and gals" that we have read about from the Bible!

With that, Leah and I wanted to share with you four things to help you find that peace in your life. They may look like they are hard to do, but if you come to Him as a child, it's not very hard.

- Ask God for His supernatural peace.
- Confess any sins that you may have in your life.
- Ask for forgiveness.
- Invite Jesus into your heart.

The last one is really very simple. In the Old Testament, Moses shared this about God's Word:

> But the word is very near you, in your mouth and in your heart, that you may observe it.
> (Deut. 30:14 NASB)

And in the New Testament, the apostle Paul shares this:

> That if you confess with your mouth Jesus as Lord, and believe in your heart that God raised Him from the dead, you will be saved.
> (Rom. 10:9 NASB)

So, here is a simple prayer to help you, and when you pray this prayer, the peace of God, which surpasses all understanding, will guard your hearts and minds!

Dear Jesus, I need You in my life. I acknowledge that I have sinned and I come to You right now confessing that and asking your forgiveness. Thank You for dying on the cross for my sins. I believe You are the Son of God and that You rose from the dead and are alive today.

I open the door of my heart and receive You as my Savior and Lord. Thank You for forgiving my sins and giving me eternal life. Please take control of my life from here forward and make me the kind of person you want me to be. In Jesus' name I pray, Amen.

A Story of Inspiration

And we know that in all things God works for the good of those who love him, who have been called according to his purpose.

(Rom. 8:28 NIV)

When Leah and I first began the process of grieving, the Lord provided many resources to assist us in our loss, our pain, and our broken hearts. Trying to make sense of everything—our daughter's murder, the young men who took her life, their families and their

Walking Through Grief

feeling of loss, and how we would walk through this journey of grief.

Asking those all-important questions of, *What do I do now? Where do I go from here? Why did this have to happen to us?* And in time, that question of, *What does God have in store for us?*

We learned that from your greatest misery, God will birth your greatest ministry. We also found hope, healing, and encouragement from the men and women who, before us, went through similar ordeals in life and came out victorious! Those stories inspired us and gave us that hope for tomorrow.

In this chapter, we wanted to share one of those stories with you. This is a story about a man named Horatio Spafford. We were honored to have received permission from the board of directors at the Spafford Children's Center in East Jerusalem to share this with you. Here is a copy of that article from their website. You will be blessed!

Brian and Leah

THE SPAFFORD HOME

In 1871, Horatio Spafford, a prosperous lawyer and devout Christian, and his wife, Anna, were living comfortably with their four young daughters in Lake View, Chicago. In that year, the great fire broke out which devastated the entire city. For the next two years, Horatio and Anna devoted their time to welfare work amongst the refugees of the fire.

By November 1873, the Spaffords needed some respite and decided to join friends in Europe but just before their departure, Horatio was detained on business. Anna and their four daughters were persuaded to set off without him, but en route tragedy struck. The steamship they were travelling on, the *Ville du Havre*, sank after colliding with another ship in mid-ocean.

Of the hundreds on board, Anna was one of only twenty-seven people who were rescued, having been kept afloat by a piece of debris. Her daughters did not survive. Overcome with despair at the loss of her children, Anna felt strongly that she had been saved for a purpose.

In Chicago, Horatio received a tragic telegram from his wife: "Saved alone." Setting off to bring Anna home, he crossed the Atlantic and the watery grave of his four daughters. Moved by the experience, he wrote a hymn, "It Is Well with My Soul," which expressed his faith. The hymn remains one of the most popular Christian hymns in the USA.

> When peace like a river attendeth my way,
> When sorrows like sea billows roll,
> Whatever my lot,
> Thou hast taught me to say:
> It is well, it is well, with my soul.

The Spafford Home

(A facsimile copy of the original hymn, handwritten by Horatio, can be downloaded from the Library of Congress website.)

Having returned to Chicago, the Spaffords were blessed with further children—a son, Horatio, and a daughter, Bertha. However, another crushing blow was dealt when little Horatio died of scarlet fever at the age of three.

The couple's faith remained strong in the face of these difficult times; but Horatio gradually became convinced that the "end of days" was imminent and decided to make a pilgrimage to the Holy Land. In a letter to a friend, Horatio explained, "Jerusalem is where my Lord lived, suffered, and conquered, and I, too, wish to learn how to live, to suffer, and especially, to conquer."

Six months after the birth of another daughter, Grace, the Spaffords and a few friends set off for Jerusalem, arriving there in September 1881. The group settled in a house in the Old City that was built against the northern medieval city wall. They came to be known as the American Colony.

From the beginning, they were generous sharing what little they had with others, and the American Colony quickly became known as a place of hospitality for all—Jews, Christians, and Muslims were all welcome there.

When they were joined later by a group of Swedish Christians, they needed larger premises and were able to move to a former Arab Pasha's home, north of the Damascus gate, where they continued their communal way of life.

During World War I, when famine and plague ravaged the city, the American Colony operated a soup kitchen for the poor of Jerusalem and also ran, with permission from the Turkish governor, hospitals for the wounded of both sides in the conflict.

Bertha Spafford Vester

On Christmas Eve of 1925, Horatio's and Anna's daughter, Bertha Spafford Vester, was hurrying home to join her husband and children to go to Bethlehem to sing carols, when she encountered a bedouin who had travelled for six hours with his sick wife and their newborn baby on a donkey. They had found the hospital closed to outpatients because of the Christmas feast. Bertha was greatly moved by their need and later said, "Here before me stood a rustic Madonna and babe, and, similar to Mary's plight, there was no place for them to stay."

She immediately took action, and the woman was admitted to the hospital. But by morning, she had died. The next day, the husband came with his baby and begged Bertha to keep the child. He said, "If I take my baby boy to my cave home, he will surely die." Bertha took the baby, named him *Noel*, hired a nurse, and established them in the house on the wall where the American Colony had first settled when they arrived in Jerusalem. Within a week, Bertha had been asked to take in two more orphaned babies.

Thus, the Spafford Baby Home was born.

Several years later, the baby home developed into a children's hospital with sixty beds and a surgical wing. For many years, it was the only children's hospital in the Old City of Jerusalem, and from 1948, it played a vital role in serving families of all faiths from Eastern Jerusalem and its surrounding villages and towns.

Adapting to Different Needs

In 1967, when Israel occupied the West Bank and East Jerusalem, it was decided that the needs of the local people could best be served by focusing on preventive medicine. The hospital was renamed the Spafford Children's Center and operated as an outpatient medical clinic for sick children, an antenatal clinic, and an infant welfare department to monitor babies well for development, weighing, and vaccinations.

The Spafford Children's Center is still located in the original American Colony home and is run as a not-for-profit organization. Some of the members of the charity's board of trustees are the great-grandchildren of Horatio and Anna Spafford whose aim remains to provide medical and social services to the local people according to their needs and the funds available.

As well as its strong heritage, the Spafford Children's Center is a forward-looking and highly professional organisation which is recognized locally as a center of excellence. The turbulent situation in the Middle East requires the Spafford Children's Center to adapt to meet each new challenge facing the families of East Jerusalem and the West Bank.

Through a program of activities and summer camps, the center offers the opportunity for youngsters from deprived backgrounds to experience normal life, which they have been denied due to the political circumstances they find themselves in.

The center has pioneered the use of new techniques in dealing with trauma and now operates growing social work and psychological departments to help families cope with the damaging effects of violence and the restrictive occupation experienced by many children in the region. The schooling of these children has also suffered, and the center helps them with remedial education classes to bring them back into the education system.

The center now also operates medical outreach programs in the West Bank, in Taybeh and Bethany (Izzariyeh), to provide services to patients who are isolated east of Israel's separation wall.

Continuing with the Same Values

Although current needs are different from those experienced when the Spafford family first came to Jerusalem, the moving spirit is still the same.

Help is given to anyone in need, regardless of race, religion, or cultural background. The center is unusual, in an area of sectarian conflict, in having staff of different faiths working together for a common cause—the benefit of deprived and sick children.

Further information on the historical events which led to the formation of the Spafford Children's Center can be obtained from the US Library of Congress (http://www.loc.gov/exhibits/americancolony/amcolony-family.html) or from reading *Our Jerusalem*, a personal account by Bertha Spafford Vester.

Wasn't that an awesome story of inspiration! Even when events in your life take a turn for the worse, God will pick you up out of the ashes and give you a vision to be used for His purpose. We have found that by being open, willing, and obedient to be used by Him, He will place us in the lives of others to encourage them on their road to recovery.

The Spafford Home

Know that God loves you, and that people are praying for you as you begin walking through grief.

> And the peace of God which surpasses all understanding, shall keep your hearts, your minds through Christ Jesus.
>
> (Phil. 4:7 NKJV)

Finding Your Next Assignment

For I know the plans I have for you declares the Lord, plans to prosper you and not to harm you, plans to give you hope and a future.

(Jer. 29:11 NIV)

I shared our story in the previous chapter about being inspired and making an impact in people's lives. Yes, the Lord brought us out of the ashes and from misery he birthed our newest ministry.

Leah and I want you to be encouraged and know that it does not matter what you do now or what you think you may do later. God has a plan already in store for you now.

He has a plan for your life, and if you do not know what it is, ask Him, and He will reveal it to you!

I love what Myles Munroe said about your gift:

> How is the fulfillment of vision meant to work in practical terms? Proverbs 18:16 (NKJV) is a powerful statement that reveals the answer: A man's gift makes room for him. What you were designed to be known for is your gift. God has put a gift or talent in every person that the world will make room for. It is this gift that will enable you to fulfill your vision. It will make a way for you in life. It is in exercising this gift that you will find real fulfillment, purpose, and contentment in your work. It is interesting to note that the Bible does not say that a man's education makes room for him, but that his gift does.

When you find out what that gift is, be prepared! You will need to be open, willing, and obedient to be used by God.

Finding Your Next Assignment

But Brian, why? you might wonder and ask. Because you see, my friend, God is preparing *you* for your next assignment in life.

It's time to seek Him and find out what your next assignment is in life. Last time I looked, there is nothing mentioned in the Bible about retiring. So we are to work and be fruitful. At one time or another, we all have been able to do certain things. Some things are better than most. But in time, due to our age, eyesight, or physical health, we will not be able to do some of the things we once did. And we may have been "retired" early from our employers or other circumstances.

But what is it that you were made to do and what things are you able to do, that you do not know that you can do? From your experience, in your loss, the Lord will show you things that you can do. These will become kingdom projects, and you will have a new attitude of gratitude when you do something new.

Yes, it may mean going back to the same job or career, but there is a new light and a new reason, and it might be only for a season. Maybe you start becoming active or more active in your church, taking a leadership role, helping children or youth, or even providing assistance to the elderly or others who need your help.

With God's help, you will begin to learn to do new things, providing help and services to those who are in need.

Lord, open my eyes that I may see what you have for me to do. What would you have me to do?

Your next assignment is just around the corner! Be encouraged!

Order Information

REDEMPTION
P R E S S

To order additional copies of this book, please visit
www.redemption-press.com.
Also available on Amazon.com and
BarnesandNoble.com
Or by calling toll free 1-844-2REDEEM.